Alborada *Shawl*

SKILL LEVEL

INTERMEDIATE

FINISHED SIZE
One size fits most

FINISHED GARMENT MEASUREMENTS
Width: 64 inches across top edge
Length: 44 inches from top edge to bottom point

MATERIALS
- Tahki Stacy Charles Cotton Classic Lite fine (sport) weight cotton yarn (1¾ oz/146 yds/50g per skein): 12 skeins #4912 red-violet
- Size D/3/3.25mm crochet hook

GAUGE
Gauge is not important for this project.

PATTERN NOTES
When body of Shawl is complete, do not fasten off, as Edging is worked along Shawl's sides.

Join with slip stitch as indicated unless otherwise stated.

SPECIAL STITCHES
2-double crochet cluster (2-dc cl): Holding back last lp of each st on hook, 2 dc in indicated st or sp, yo, draw through all 3 lps on hook.

3-double crochet cluster (3-dc cl): Holding back last lp of each st on hook, 3 dc in indicated st or sp, yo, draw through all 4 lps on hook.

Cluster shell (cl shell): (3-dc cl— *see Special Stitches*, ch 2, 3-dc cl) in indicated st or sp.

Beginning cluster shell (beg cl shell): Ch 3, **2-dc cl** (*see Special Stitches*), ch 2, 3-dc cl in same st or sp.

Picot: Ch 3, insert hook in 3rd ch from hook, yo and draw yarn through, yo and draw through 2 lps on hook.

SHAWL
BODY

Row 1: Ch 7 and **join** (*see Pattern Notes*) in first ch to form a ring, ch 3, **2-dc cl** (*see Special Stitches*) in ring, [ch 2, **3-dc cl** (*see Special Stitches*) in ring] 5 times, turn. (*6 cls, 5 ch-2 sps*)

Row 2: Sl st in first ch-2 sp, **beg cl shell** (*see Special Stitches*) in same ch sp, ch 1, **cl shell** (*see Special Stitches*) in next ch-2 sp, ch 1, 7 dc in next ch-2 sp (*pineapple base made*), [ch 1, cl shell in next ch-2 sp] twice, turn. (*4 cl shells, 1 pineapple base*)

Row 3: Sl st in first ch-2 sp, beg cl shell in same ch sp, ch 2, cl shell in next ch-2 sp, ch 2, sk next ch, [dc in next dc, ch 1] 7 times, ch 1, sk next ch, [cl shell in next ch-2 sp, ch 2] twice, turn. (*4 cl shells, 4 ch-2 sps, 6 ch-1 sps, 7 dc*)

Row 4: Sl st in first ch-2 sp, beg cl shell in same ch sp, ch 3, sk next ch sp, cl shell in next ch-2 sp, ch 3, sk (ch-2 sp, dc), [sc in next ch-1 sp, ch 3, sk next dc] 6 times, sk next ch-2 sp, cl shell in next ch-2 sp, ch 3, cl shell in last ch-2 sp, turn. (*4 cl shells, 6 sc, 9 ch-3 sps*)

Row 5: Sl st in first ch-2 sp, beg cl shell in same ch sp, ch 3, sk next ch sp, (cl shell, ch 2, 3-dc cl) in next ch-2 sp, ch 3, sk next ch-3 sp, sc in next ch-3 sp, [ch 3, sc in next ch-3 sp] 4 times, ch 3, sk next ch sp, (cl shell, ch 2, 3-dc cl) in next ch-2 sp, ch 3, sk next ch sp, cl shell in last ch-2 sp, turn. (*10 3-dc cls, 8 ch-3 sps, 6 ch-2 sps, 5 sc*)

Row 6: Sl st in first ch-2 sp, beg cl shell in same ch sp, ch 3, sk next ch sp, [cl shell in next ch-2 sp, ch 2] twice, ch 1, sk next (ch sp, sc), [sc in next ch-3 sp, ch 3] 4 times, sk next ch sp, [cl shell in next ch-2 sp, ch 2] twice, ch 1, sk next ch sp, cl shell in last ch-2 sp, turn. (*6 cl shells, 7 ch-3 sps, 4 sc*)

Row 7: Sl st in first ch-2 sp, beg cl shell in same ch sp, ch 3, sk next ch sp, [cl shell in next ch-2 sp, ch 2] 3 times, ch 1, sk next (ch sp, sc), [sc in next ch-3 sp, ch 3] 3 times, sk next ch sp, [cl shell in next ch-2 sp, ch 2] 3 times, ch 1, sk next ch sp, cl shell in last ch-2 sp, turn. (*8 cl shells, 6 ch-3 sps, 3 sc*)

Row 8: Sl st in first ch-2 sp, beg cl shell in same ch sp, ch 3, [cl shell in ch sp of next cl shell, ch 3] 3 times, sk next (ch sp, sc), [sc in next ch-3 sp, ch 3] twice, [cl shell in ch sp of next cl shell, ch 3] 3 times, cl shell in last ch-2 sp, turn. (*8 cl shells, 9 ch-3 sps, 2 sc*)

Row 9: Sl st in first ch-2 sp, beg cl shell in same ch sp, ch 3, cl shell in ch sp of next cl shell, ch 1, 7 dc in ch sp of next cl shell (*pineapple base made*), ch 1, cl shell in ch sp of next cl shell, ch 3, sk next (ch sp, sc), sc in next ch-3 sp, ch 3, cl shell in ch sp of next cl shell, ch 1, 7 dc in ch sp of next cl shell (*pineapple base made*), ch 1, cl shell in ch sp of next cl shell, ch 3, cl shell in last ch-2 sp, turn. (*6 cl shells, 2 pineapple bases, 1 sc*)

Row 10: Sl st in first ch-2 sp, beg cl shell in same ch sp, ch 3, cl shell in ch sp of next cl shell, ch 2, [dc in next dc, ch 1] 7 times, ch 2, cl shell in ch sp of each of next 2 cl shells, ch 3, [dc in next dc, ch 1] 7 times, ch 2, cl shell in ch sp of next cl shell, ch 3, cl shell in last ch-2 sp, turn. (*6 cl shells, 14 dc*)

Row 11: Sl st in first ch-2 sp, beg cl shell in same ch sp, ch 3, cl shell in next cl shell, *ch 3, sk next (ch sp, dc), [sc in next ch-1 sp, ch 3] 6 times*, cl shell in each of next 2 cl shells, rep between * once, cl shell in next cl shell, ch 3, cl shell in last cl shell, turn. (*6 cl shells, 12 dc*)

Row 12: Sl st in first ch-2 sp, beg cl shell in same ch sp, ch 3, [cl shell, ch 2, 3-dc cl] in next cl shell, *ch 3, sk next (ch sp, sc), [sc in next ch sp, ch 3] 5 times*, [cl shell in next cl shell] twice, rep between * once, [cl shell, ch 2, 3-dc cl] in next cl shell, ch 3, cl shell in last cl shell, turn. (*10 sc, 14 3-dc cls*)

Row 13: Sl st in first ch-2 sp, beg cl shell in same ch sp, ch 3, sk next ch sp, [cl shell in next ch-2 sp, ch 2] twice, ch 1, *sk next (ch sp, sc), [sc in next ch sp, ch 3] 4 times*, [cl shell in next cl shell, ch 3] twice, rep between * once, sk next ch sp, [cl shell in next ch-2 sp, ch 2] twice, ch 1, sk next ch sp, cl shell in last cl shell, turn. (*8 sc, 8 cl shells*)

Row 14: Sl st in first ch-2 sp, beg cl shell in same ch sp, ch 3, sk next ch sp, (cl shell, ch 2) in each of next 3 ch-2 sps, ch 1, *sk next (ch sp, sc), [sc in next ch sp, ch 3] 3 times*, sk next ch sp, [cl shell in next ch sp, ch 2] 3 times, ch 1, sk next ch sp, rep between *, sk next ch sp, [cl shell, ch 2] in each of next 3 ch-2 sps, ch 1, cl shell in last cl shell, turn. (*11 cl shells, 6 sc*)

Row 15: Sl st in first ch-2 sp, beg cl shell in same ch sp, *[ch 3, cl shell in next cl shell] 3 times, ch 3**, sk next (ch sp, sc), sc in next ch sp, ch 3, sc in next ch sp, rep from * 3 times, ending last rep at **, cl shell in last cl shell, turn. (*11 cl shells, 4 sc*)

Row 16: Sl st in first ch-2 sp, beg cl shell in same ch sp, *ch 3, sk next ch sp, cl shell in next cl shell, ch 1, 7 dc in next cl shell (*pineapple base made*), ch 1, cl shell in next cl shell, ch 3, sk next ch sp**, sc in next ch sp, rep from * across ending last rep at **, cl shell in last cl shell, turn. (*8 cl shells, 2 sc, 3 pineapple bases*)

Row 17: Sl st in first ch-2 sp, beg cl shell in same ch sp, ch 3, sk next ch sp, *cl shell in next cl shell, ch 2, [dc in next dc, ch 1] 6 times, dc in next dc, ch 2, cl shell in next cl shell, rep from * twice, ch 3, cl shell in last cl shell, turn. (*8 cl shells, 21 dc, 18 ch-1 sps*)

Row 18: Sl st in first ch-2 sp, beg cl shell in same ch sp, ch 3, *cl shell in next cl shell, ch 3, sk next (ch sp, dc), [sc in next ch-1 sp, ch 3] 6 times, cl shell in next cl shell, rep from * across to last cl shell, ch 3, cl shell in last cl shell. (*8 cl shells, 18 sc*)

Row 19: Sl st in first ch-2 sp, beg cl shell in same ch sp, ch 3, (cl shell, ch 2, 3-dc cl) in next cl shell, *ch 3, sk next (ch sp, sc), [sc in next ch-3 sp, ch 3] 5 times**, cl shell in each of next 2 cl shells, rep from * across, ending last rep at **, (cl shell, ch 2, 3-dc cl) in next cl shell, ch 3, cl shell in last cl shell, turn. (*8 cl shells, 2 3-dc cls, 15 sc*)

Row 20: Sl st in first ch-2 sp, beg cl shell in same ch sp, ch 3, [cl shell in next ch-2 sp, ch 2] twice, ch 1, *sk next (ch sp, sc), [sc in next ch-3 sp, ch 3] 4 times**, cl shell in next cl shell, ch 2, cl shell in next cl shell, ch 3, rep from *, ending last rep at **, [cl shell in next ch-2 sp, ch 2] twice, ch 1, cl shell in last cl shell, turn. *(10 cl shells, 12 sc)*

Row 21: Sl st in first ch-2 sp, beg cl shell in same ch sp, ch 3, * sk next ch sp, [cl shell in next ch-2 sp, ch 2] 3 times, ch 1**, sk next (ch sp, sc), [sc in next ch-3 sp, ch 3] 3 times, rep from * across, ending rep at **, cl shell in last cl shell, turn. *(14 cl shells, 9 sc)*

Row 22: Sl st in first ch-2 sp, beg cl shell in same ch sp, ch 3, *[cl shell in next cl shell, ch 3] 3 times**, sk next (ch sp, sc), [sc in next ch-3 sp, ch 3] twice, rep from * across, ending last rep at ** before last 2 ch sp, cl shell in last cl shell, turn. *(14 cl shells, 6 sc)*

Row 23: Sl st in first ch-2 sp, beg cl shell in same ch sp, ch 3, *cl shell in next cl shell, ch 1, 7 dc in next cl shell *(pineapple base made)*, ch 1, cl shell in next cl shell, ch 3**, sk next (ch sp, sc), sc in next ch-3 sp, ch 3, rep from * across, ending last rep at **, cl shell in last cl shell, turn. *(10 cl shells, 3 sc, 4 pineapple bases)*

Row 24: Sl st in first ch-2 sp, beg cl shell in same ch sp, ch 3, *cl shell in next cl shell, ch 2, [dc in next dc, ch 1] 6 times, dc in next dc, ch 2, cl shell in next cl shell**, sk next (ch-3 sp, sc, ch-3 sp), rep from * across, ending last rep at **, ch 3, cl shell in last cl shell. *(10 cl shells, 28 dc, 24 ch-1 sps)*

Rows 25–93: Rep rows 18–24, ending with row 23. *(14 pineapple bases at end of last row)*

Row 94: Sl st in first ch-2 sp, beg cl shell in same ch sp, ch 3, *cl shell in next cl shell, ch 2, [dc in next dc, ch 1] 6 times, dc in next dc, ch 2, cl shell in next cl shell**, sk next (ch-3 sp, sc, ch-3 sp), rep from * across, ending last rep at **, ch 3, cl shell in last cl shell. *(30 cl shells, 98 dc)*

Row 95: Sl st in first ch-2 sp, beg cl shell in same ch sp, ch 3, *cl shell in next cl shell, ch 3, sk next (ch sp, dc), [3-dc cl in next ch-1 sp, ch 2] 6 times, ch 1, cl shell in next cl shell, rep from * across to last cl shell, ch 3, cl shell in last cl shell, turn. *(30 cl shells, 84 3-dc cls)*

Row 96: Sl st in first ch-2 sp, ch 1, 2 sc in same ch sp, **picot** *(see Special Stitches)*, 2 sc in same ch sp, (2 sc, picot, 2 sc) in each ch sp across, sl st in last dc. Do not fasten off.

Turn work 90 degrees counterclockwise to begin working Edging along left side toward point.

EDGING
Row 97: *Ch 10, 3-dc cl in 4th ch from hook, ch 3, pinch 3-dc cl and ch lps and rotate a ½ turn, sc around ch at base of 3-dc cl, ch 6, skip next 2 sps formed by cl shell, sc in next sp formed by cl shell, rep from * along edge to point, being sure to work sc in beg ring between 2 3-dc cls, continue along right edge away from point, ending with sc in last dc of last cl shell. Fasten off. *(64 bobbles)*

FINISHING
Weave in ends and block. ∎

Art Deco Shawl

SKILL LEVEL
■■■□
INTERMEDIATE

FINISHED SIZES
One size fits most

FINISHED GARMENT MEASUREMENTS
Width: 60 inches across top edge
Length: 29 inches from top edge
to bottom point

MATERIALS
- Cascade Ultra Pima Cotton (fine) sport weight cotton yarn (3½ oz/220 yds/ 100g per skein):
  6 skeins #3718 ecru
- Size D/3/3.25mm crochet hook

GAUGE
Gauge is not important for this project.

PATTERN NOTES
Weave in ends as work progresses.

Chain-3 at beginning of row or round counts as first double crochet unless otherwise stated.

Chain-6 at beginning of row or round counts as first double crochet and chain-3 sp unless otherwise stated.

Join with slip stitch as indicated unless otherwise stated.

When told to work in shell, work in chain space of shell unless otherwise stated.

SPECIAL STITCHES

Picot: Ch 3, insert hook in 3rd ch from hook, yo and draw yarn through st and lp on hook.

Shell: (2 dc, ch 2, 2 dc), in indicated st or sp.

Double crochet popcorn (dc pc): 6 dc in indicated st, drop lp, insert hook into first dc of 6-dc group and pick up dropped lp, draw through dc.

Beginning double crochet popcorn (beg dc pc): 5 dc in lp, drop lp, insert hook into top of beg ch-3 and pick up dropped lp, draw through dc.

SHAWL
BODY

Row 1: Ch 6, **join** (*see Pattern Notes*) in 6th ch from hook to form a ring, **ch 3** (*see Pattern Notes*), dc in ring, (ch 2, 2 dc) 3 times in ring, turn. (8 dc, 3 ch sps)

Row 2: Ch 3, **shell** (*see Special Stitches*) in next ch-2 sp, [ch 2, shell in next ch sp] twice, turn. (3 shells)

Row 3: Ch 3, shell in next ch sp, *ch 5, (sc, ch 3, sc) in next ch sp, ch 5, shell in next ch sp, rep from * across, turn. (3 shells, 4 ch-5 sps, 4 sc, 2 ch-3 sps)

Row 4: Ch 3, shell in next ch sp, *ch 5, (sc, ch 3, sc) in next ch-5 sp*, rep between * across to center shell, ch 5, shell **in center shell** (*see Pattern Notes*), rep between * across to last shell, ch 5, shell in last shell, turn.

Rows 5–34: Rep rnd 4. At end of last row, fasten off and weave in ends. Gently steam block.

LARGE MOTIF
MAKE 6.

Rnd 1: Ch 6, join in 6th ch from hook to form ring, ch 3 *(does not count as a dc)*, **beg dc pc** *(see Special Stitches)* in ring, [ch 3, **dc pc** *(see Special Stitches)* in ring] 5 times, ch 3, join in top of beg dc pc. *(6 dc pc)*

Rnd 2: Ch 3, 5 dc in ch-3 sp, [6 dc in next ch-3 sp] 5 times, join in top of ch-3. *(36 dc)*

Rnd 3: Ch 1, sc in **back lp** *(see Stitch Guide)* of same ch as joining, working in back lps, sc in each st around, join in first st. *(36 sc)*

Rnd 4: Ch 2, working in back lps, **dc dec** *(see Stitch Guide)* in next 2 sts, [ch 4, dc dec in next 3 sts] 11 times, sk beg ch 2, join in next st. *(12 sts)*

Rnd 5: Ch 1, *7 dc in next ch-4 sp, sc in next st, rep from * around, join in beg ch-1. *(84 dc, 12 sc)*

Rnd 6: Ch 6 *(see Pattern Notes)*, *sk next 3 dc, sc in next dc, ch 3, sk 3 dc, dc in next sc, ch 3, rep from * across, join in beg ch-6 sp. *(24 ch-3 sp)*

Rnd 7: Ch 1, sc in same sp as joining, ch 5, *sc in next ch-3 sp, ch 5, rep from * around, join in first sc. *(24 ch-5 sp)*

Rnd 8: Sl st in each of next 2 chs, ch 1, sc in same sp, ch 5, *sc in next ch-5 sp, ch 5, rep from * around, join in first sc.

Rnd 9: Sl st in next 2 chs, ch 1, sc in same ch-5 sp, *ch 2, sk next sc, (3 dc, **picot**—*see Special Stitches*, 3 dc) in next ch-5 sp, ch 2, sk next sc**, sc in next ch sp, rep from * around ending last rep at **, join in first sc of round. Fasten off. *(12 shells with picot tips)*

MEDIUM MOTIF
MAKE 32.

Rnd 1: Ch 6, join in 6th ch from hook to form ring, ch 3 *(does not count as a dc)*, beg dc pc in ring, [ch 3, dc pc in ring] 5 times, ch 3, join in top of first dc pc. *(6 dc pc)*

Rnd 2: Ch 1, *(3 dc, picot, 3 dc) in next ch sp**, sc in next dc pc, rep from * around, ending at ** on last rep, join in first ch-1. Fasten off. *(6 shells with picot tips)*

SMALL MOTIF
MAKE 43.
Work rnd 1 of Medium Motif. Fasten off.

ASSEMBLY
Referring to Assembly Diagram, attach Motifs to Body. ■

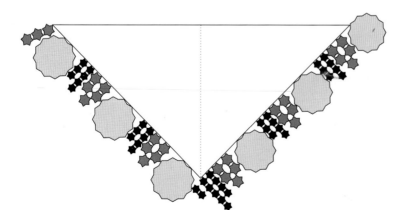

Art Deco Shawl
Motif Assembly Diagram

MOTIF KEY

Large motif

Medium motif

Small motif

Celtic Nature

SKILL LEVEL

INTERMEDIATE

FINISHED SIZE
One size fits most

FINISHED GARMENT MEASUREMENTS
Width: 58 inches across top edge
Length: 23 inches from top edge to bottom point

MATERIALS
- Universal Nazli Gelin Garden 3 (fine) size 3 crochet cotton (1¾ oz/136 yds/50g per ball): 8 balls #300-16 medium sage
- Size D/3/3.25mm crochet hook
- 12 stitch markers

GAUGE
Gauge is not important for this project.

PATTERN NOTES
Motifs are joined as you go. Two motifs are joined on 2 sides (M2); 3 motifs are joined on 3 sides (M3); 10 motifs are joined on 4 sides (M4); 1 motif is joined on 5 sides (M5); 5 motifs are joined on 6 sides (M6). Instructions for round 8 are given for M6. Instructions for joining edges are given separately. Refer to Assembly Diagram when joining motifs. Alternatively, work motifs separately and sew together.

Chain-3 at beginning of round counts as first double crochet unless otherwise stated.

Join with slip stitch as indicated unless otherwise stated.

SPECIAL STITCHES
Cluster (cl): Keeping last lp of each st on hook, 3 dc in indicated st or sp, yo, draw through all 4 lps on hook.

Cluster shell (cl shell): Work (**cl**—*see Special Stitches,* ch 2, cl) in indicated st or sp.

Beginning cluster shell (beg cl shell): Ch 3, holding last lp of each st on hook, 2 dc in indicated st or sp, ch 2, cl in same st or sp.

Picot: Ch 3, insert hook in 3rd ch from hook, yo and draw yarn through, yo and draw through 2 lps on hook.

SHAWL
LARGE MOTIF
MAKE 21.
Rnd 1: Ch 6 and **join** *(see Pattern Notes)* in first ch to form a ring, **ch 3** *(does not count as a st),* 24 dc in ring, join in top of beg ch-3. *(24 dc)*

Rnd 2: Ch 1, *sc in **back lp** *(see Stitch Guide)* of next st, (sc, ch 3, sc) in back lp of next st, rep from * 11 times, join in first ch. *(36 sc, 12 ch-3 lps)*

Rnd 3: *Ch 12, sk (sc, ch-3 sp, sc), sc in next sc, rep from * 10 times, ch 6, sk (sc, ch-3 sp, sc), **dtr** *(see Stitch Guide) in* first ch of beg ch-12. *(12 ch-12 lps)*

Rnd 4: **Beg cl shell** (*see Special Stitches*) in first ch-12 sp, ch 3, *cl shell (*see Special Stitches*) in next ch-12 sp, ch 3, rep from * 10 times, join in top of first cl. (*12 cl shells, 12 ch-3 sps*)

Rnd 5: Sl st in first ch-2 sp, beg cl shell in same sp, ch 3, sc in next ch-3 sp, ch 3, *cl shell in next ch-2 sp of center cl shell, ch 3, sc in next ch-3 sp, ch 3, rep from * 10 times, join in top of first cl.

Rnd 6: Sl st in first ch-2 sp, beg cl shell in same sp, ch 3, sc in next sc, ch 3, *cl shell in ch-2 sp of next cl shell, ch 3, sc in next sc, ch 3, rep from * 10 times, join in top of first cl.

Rnd 7: Rep rnd 6.

MOTIF M6 ONLY
Rnd 8: Sl st in first ch-2 sp, ch 3, **picot** (*see Special Stitches*), dc in same ch-sp, picot, [dc in same ch-sp, picot, place stitch marker in picot] twice, [dc in same ch-sp, picot] twice, *ch 2, sk (cl, ch-3 sp), sc in next sc, ch 2, sk (ch-3 sp, cl), ◊[dc in ch-2 sp, picot] twice, [dc in same ch sp, picot, place stitch marker in picot] twice, [dc in same ch sp, picot] twice◊, rep from * 10 times, ch 2, sk (cl, ch-3 sp), sc in next sc, ch 2, sk ch-3 sp, join in first cl. (*72 dc, 72 picots, 12 sc, 24 ch-2 sps, 24 marked picots*)

MOTIFS M2, M3, M4 & M5 ONLY
Work rnd 8 as above, but place stitch markers only on edges to be joined that have not already been joined and leave rest of picots unmarked.

JOINING EDGE
Work rnd 8 as above, but replace instructions between ◊◊ twice for each edge when joining to another motif as follows: ◊[dc in ch-2 sp, picot] twice, [dc in ch-2 sp, ch 1, sc in marked picot of neighboring motif, ch 1] twice, [dc in same ch sp, picot] twice◊. See Assembly Diagram on page 10 for which edges to join.

SMALL MOTIF
MAKE 10.
Rnd 1: Ch 6 and join in first ch to form a ring, ch 3 (*does not count as a dc*), 24 dc into ring, join in top of ch-3.

Rnd 2: Ch 1, *sc in back lp of next st, (sc, ch 3, sc) in back lp of next st, rep from * around, join in first ch-1. *(12 ch-3 lps, 36 sc)*

JOINING CHAIN
Ch 12, join in side of sc that connects two Large Motifs in seams indicated in Assembly Diagram. Fasten off.

FINISHING
Weave in all ends and steam block. ■

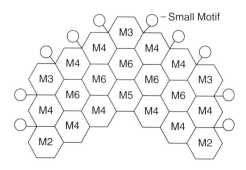

Celtic Nature Shawl
Motif Assembly Diagram

MOTIF KEY	
(M2)	Motif 2
(M3)	Motif 3
(M4)	Motif 4
(M5)	Motif 5
(M6)	Motif 6

Galician Sea Shawl

SKILL LEVEL

INTERMEDIATE

FINISHED SIZE
One size fits most

FINISHED GARMENT MEASUREMENTS
Width: 77 inches across top edge
Length: 36 inches from top edge to bottom point

MATERIALS
- Omega Sinfonia light (light worsted) weight cotton yarn (3½ oz/232 yds/ 100g per ball):
    5 balls #816 teal
- Size D/3/3.25mm crochet hook

GAUGE
Gauge is not important for this project.

PATTERN NOTES
Chain-3 at beginning of row counts as first double crochet unless otherwise stated.

Join with slip stitch as indicated unless otherwise stated.

When told to work in shell, work in chain space of shell unless otherwise stated.

SPECIAL STITCHES
Shell: (3 dc, ch 2, 3 dc) in indicated st or sp.

3-treble crochet cluster (3-tr cl): Holding back last lp of each st on hook, 3 tr in indicated st or sp, yo, draw through all 4 lps on hook.

Picot: Ch 3, insert hook in 3rd ch from hook, yo and draw yarn through, yo and draw yarn through 2 lps on hook.

SHAWL
BODY
Row 1: Ch 6 and **join** (*see Pattern Notes*) in 6th ch from hook to form ring, **ch 3** (*see Pattern Notes*), 2 dc in ring, (ch 2, 3 dc, ch 5, 3 dc) twice in ring, ch 2, 3 dc, turn. (*18 dc, 5 ch sps*)

Row 2: Ch 3, sk next 2 dc, **shell** (*see Special Stitches*) in ch-2 sp, [ch 5, sk next 3 dc, (sc, ch 5, sc) in next ch-5 sp, ch 5, sk next 3 dc, shell in ch-2 sp] twice, turn. (*3 shells, 2 ch-5 sps*)

Row 3: Ch 3, shell in first ch-2 sp, *ch 5, sc in next ch-5 sp, ch 5, sk next ch-5 sp, sc in next ch-5 sp, ch 5, shell **in next shell** (*see Pattern Notes*), rep from * once, turn. (*3 shells, 6 ch-5 sps*)

Row 4: Ch 3, shell in first ch-2 sp, *ch 5, sc in next ch-5 sp, 9 dc in next ch-5 sp, sc in next ch-5 sp, ch 5, shell in next shell, rep from * once, turn. (*3 shells, 4 sc, 18 dc, 4 ch-5 sps*)

Row 5: Ch 3, shell in first ch-2 sp, *ch 5, (sc, ch 5, sc) in next ch-5 sp, ch 5, sk next 3 dc, sc in each of next 3 dc, ch 5, sk next 3 dc, (sc, ch 5, sc) in next ch-5 sp, ch 5, shell in next shell, rep from * once, turn.

Row 6: Ch 3, shell in first ch-2 sp, *ch 5, sc in next ch-5 sp, ch 5, sk next ch-5 sp, sc in next ch-5 sp, **ch 3, sc in next sc, ch 3, sc in ch-5 sp, ch 5, sk next ch-5 sp, sc in ch-5 sp, rep from ** to next shell, ch 5, shell in next shell, rep from * across, turn.

Row 7: Ch 3, shell in first ch-2 sp, *ch 5, sc in next ch-5 sp, 9 dc in next ch-5 sp, sc in next ch-3 sp, ch 3, sc in next ch-3 sp, 9 dc in next ch-5 sp, sc in next ch-5 sp, ch 5, shell in next shell, rep from * once, turn.

Row 8: Ch 3, shell in first ch-2 sp, ch 5, (sc, ch 5, sc) in next ch-5 sp, ch 5, *sk next 3 dc, sc in each of next 3 dc, ch 5, (sc, ch 5, sc) in next ch-5 sp, ch 5*, rep between * to next shell, shell in next shell, ch 5, (sc, ch 5, sc) in next ch-5 sp, ch 5, rep between * to last shell, shell in last shell, turn.

Row 9: Ch 3, shell in first ch-2 sp, *ch 5, sc in next ch-5 sp, ch 5, sk next ch-5 sp, **sc in next ch-5 sp, ch 3, sk next sc, sc in next sc, ch 3, sc in next ch-5 sp, ch 5, sk next ch-5 sp **, rep between ** to ch-5 sp before next shell, sc in next ch-5 sp, ch 5, shell in next shell, rep from * once, turn.

Row 10: Ch 3, shell in first ch-2 sp, *ch 5, sc in next ch sp, **9 dc in next ch-5 sp, sc in next ch-3 sp, ch 3, sc in next ch-3 sp**, rep between ** to last 2 ch-5 sps before next shell, 9 dc in next ch-5 sp, sc in next ch-5 sp, ch 5, shell in next shell, rep from * once, turn.

Rows 11–67: [Rep rows 8–10] 19 times.

RUFFLE
Row 68: Sl st in each of next 2 dc, sc in next ch-2 sp, *ch 10, sk next ch-5 sp and next 3 dc, sc in each of next 3 dc, rep from * to next shell, ch 10, sc in ch-2 sp of next shell, **ch 10, sk next ch-5 sp and next 3 dc, sc in each of next 3 dc, rep from * to last shell, ch 10, sc in ch-2 sp of shell shell, turn. (*46 10-sps*)

Row 69: **Ch 3** (*see Pattern Notes*), 14 dc in ch-10 sp, *sk next sc, sc in next sc, sk next sc, 15 dc in next ch-10 sp, rep from * 21 times, sc in next sc, 15 dc in next ch-10 sp, **sk next sc, sc in next sc, 15 dc in next ch-10 sp, rep from ** 21 times, sc in last sc, turn.

Row 70: Sl st in each of next 4 dc, ch 1, sc in each of next 7 dc, *ch 3, sk next 4 dc, (dc, ch 5, dc) in next sc, ch 3, sk next 4 dc, sc in each of next 7 dc, rep from * across, turn.

Row 71: Sl st in first sc, sc in each of next 5 sts, *sk next (sc, ch-3 sp), 15 tr in next ch-5 sp, sk next (ch-3 sp, sc), sc in each of next 5 sts, rep from * across, turn.

Row 72: Sl st in first sc, ch 4, **tr dec** (*see Stitch Guide*) in next 2 sts, *ch 3, sk next sc and next 3 tr, **3-tr cl** (*see Special Stitches*) in next st, [ch 3, sk next st, 3-tr cl in next st] 4 times, ch 3, sk next 3 tr and next sc, tr dec in next 3 sts, rep from * across, turn.

Row 73: Sl st in next ch-3 sp, ch 3, (2 dc, **picot**— *see Special Stitches*, 3 dc) in same sp, (3 dc, picot, 3 dc) in each rem ch-3 sp across.

Fasten off.

FINISHING
Weave in ends and block. ∎

Volvoreta *Stole*

SKILL LEVEL

EASY

FINISHED SIZE
One size fits most

FINISHED GARMENT MEASUREMENTS
Width: 17½ inches
Length: 66 inches, excluding ornaments

MATERIALS
- Universal Yarn Swiss Mohair super fine (fingering) weight acrylic/mohair/nylon yarn (3½ oz/601 yds/100g per ball):
  3 balls #2503 ram
- Sizes D/3/3.25mm and G/6/4mm crochet hooks
- Fiberfill
- Yarn needle

1 SUPER FINE

GAUGE
Gauge is not important for this project; however, a lofty fabric with drape is desirable.

PATTERN NOTES
Chain-3 at beginning of row counts as first double crochet.

Join with slip stitch as indicated unless otherwise stated.

STOLE
BODY
Row 1: With size G hook, ch 108, sc in 2nd ch from hook and in each ch across, turn. *(107 sc)*

Row 2 (RS): Ch 3 *(see Pattern Notes)*, 4 dc in first sc, [sk next sc, dc in next sc] 7 times, sk next 2 sc, *11 dc in next sc, sk next 2 sc, dc in next sc, [sk next sc, dc in next sc] 6 times**, sk next 2 sc, rep from * across to last 2 sts, ending at **, sk next sc, 5 dc in last sc, turn. *(107 dc)*

Row 3: Ch 1, working in **front lps** *(see Stitch Guide)*, sc in each dc across, turn.

Rows 4–149: [Rep rows 2 & 3 alternately] 73 times. Fasten off. Weave in ends.

ORNAMENTS
MAKE 14.
Rnd 1: With size D hook, ch 4, **join** *(see Pattern Notes)* in first ch to form a ring, ch 1, 8 sc in ring, join in first sc. *(8 sc)*

Rnd 2: Ch 1, sc in same st, [2 sc in next st, sc in next st] 3 times, sc in next st, join in first sc. *(11 sc)*

Rnd 3: Ch 1, sc in each sc around, join in first sc.

Rnds 4–6: Rep rnd 3.

Rnd 7: Ch 1, sc in first st, [**sc dec** *(see Stitch Guide)* in next 2 sts] 5 times, join in first sc. *(6 sts)*

Fill Ornament with fiberfill.

Rnd 8: Ch 1, [sc dec in next 2 sts] 3 times, join in first sc. Leaving 6-inch tail, fasten off. Weave in ends.

ASSEMBLY
Thread 6-inch tail of yarn from ornament into yarn needle, run needle through tops of last 3 sts from rnd 8 and pull tight. Sew Ornaments firmly to points made by fan stitches *(7 across each end of Stole)*. ■

STITCH GUIDE

STITCH ABBREVIATIONS

beg .... begin/begins/beginning
bpdc .... back post double crochet
bpsc .... back post single crochet
bptr .... back post treble crochet
CC .... contrasting color
ch(s) .... chain(s)
ch- .... refers to chain or space
previously made (i.e., ch-1 space)
ch sp(s) .... chain space(s)
cl(s) .... cluster(s)
cm .... centimeter(s)
dc .... double crochet (singular/plural)
dc dec .... double crochet 2 or more
stitches together, as indicated
dec .... decrease/decreases/decreasing
dtr .... double treble crochet
ext .... extended
fpdc .... front post double crochet
fpsc .... front post single crochet
fptr .... front post treble crochet
g .... gram(s)
hdc .... half double crochet
hdc dec .... half double crochet 2 or more
stitches together, as indicated
inc .... increase/increases/increasing
lp(s) .... loop(s)
MC .... main color
mm .... millimeter(s)
oz .... ounce(s)
pc .... popcorn(s)
rem .... remain/remains/remaining
rep(s) .... repeat(s)
rnd(s) .... round(s)
RS .... right side
sc .... single crochet (singular/plural)
sc dec .... single crochet 2 or more
stitches together, as indicated
sk .... skip/skipped/skipping
sl st(s) .... slip stitch(es)
sp(s) .... space(s)/spaced
st(s) .... stitch(es)
tog .... together
tr .... treble crochet
trtr .... triple treble
WS .... wrong side
yd(s) .... yard(s)
yo .... yarn over

YARN CONVERSION

OUNCES TO GRAMS	GRAMS TO OUNCES
1............28.4	25..............⅞
2............56.7	40.............1⅔
3............85.0	50.............1¾
4.........113.4	100...........3½

UNITED STATES		UNITED KINGDOM
sl st (slip stitch)	=	sc (single crochet)
sc (single crochet)	=	dc (double crochet)
hdc (half double crochet)	=	htr (half treble crochet)
dc (double crochet)	=	tr (treble crochet)
tr (treble crochet)	=	dtr (double treble crochet)
dtr (double treble crochet)	=	ttr (triple treble crochet)
skip	=	miss

Single crochet decrease (sc dec): (Insert hook, yo, draw lp through) in each of the sts indicated, yo, draw through all lps on hook.

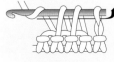

Example of 2-sc dec

Half double crochet decrease (hdc dec): (Yo, insert hook, yo, draw lp through) in each of the sts indicated, yo, draw through all lps on hook.

Example of 2-hdc dec

Reverse single crochet (reverse sc): Ch 1, sk first st, working from left to right, insert hook in next st from front to back, draw up lp on hook, yo, and draw through both lps on hook.

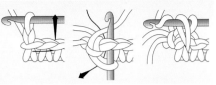

Chain (ch): Yo, pull through lp on hook.

Single crochet (sc): Insert hook in st, yo, pull through st, yo, pull through both lps on hook.

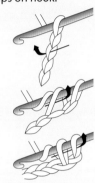

Double crochet (dc): Yo, insert hook in st, yo, pull through st, [yo, pull through 2 lps] twice.

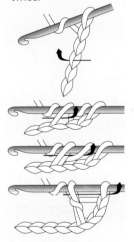

Double crochet decrease (dc dec): (Yo, insert hook, yo, draw lp through, yo, draw through 2 lps on hook) in each of the sts indicated, yo, draw through all lps on hook.

Example of 2-dc dec

Front loop (front lp) Back loop (back lp)

Front Loop   Back Loop

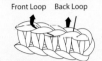

Front post stitch (fp): Back post stitch (bp): When working post st, insert hook from right to left around post of st on previous row.

Back   Front

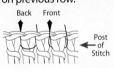

Post of Stitch

Half double crochet (hdc): Yo, insert hook in st, yo, pull through st, yo, pull through all 3 lps on hook.

Double treble crochet (dtr): Yo 3 times, insert hook in st, yo, pull through st, [yo, pull through 2 lps] 4 times.

Treble crochet decrease (tr dec): Holding back last lp of each st, tr in each of the sts indicated, yo, pull through all lps on hook.

Example of 2-tr dec

Slip stitch (sl st): Insert hook in st, pull through both lps on hook.

Chain color change (ch color change) Yo with new color, draw through last lp on hook.

Double crochet color change (dc color change) Drop first color, yo with new color, draw through last 2 lps of st.

Treble crochet (tr): Yo twice, insert hook in st, yo, pull through st, [yo, pull through 2 lps] 3 times.

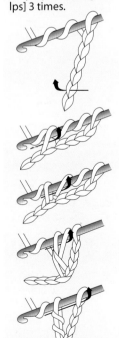

Metric
Conversion
Charts

METRIC CONVERSIONS

yards	x	.9144	=	metres (m)
yards	x	91.44	=	centimetres (cm)
inches	x	2.54	=	centimetres (cm)
inches	x	25.40	=	millimetres (mm)
inches	x	.0254	=	metres (m)

centimetres	x	.3937	=	inches
metres	x	1.0936	=	yards

INCHES INTO MILLIMETRES & CENTIMETRES (Rounded off slightly)

inches	mm	cm	inches	cm	inches	cm	inches	cm
1/8	3	0.3	5	12.5	21	53.5	38	96.5
1/4	6	0.6	5 1/2	14	22	56	39	99
3/8	10	1	6	15	23	58.5	40	101.5
1/2	13	1.3	7	18	24	61	41	104
5/8	15	1.5	8	20.5	25	63.5	42	106.5
3/4	20	2	9	23	26	66	43	109
7/8	22	2.2	10	25.5	27	68.5	44	112
1	25	2.5	11	28	28	71	45	114.5
1 1/4	32	3.2	12	30.5	29	73.5	46	117
1 1/2	38	3.8	13	33	30	76	47	119.5
1 3/4	45	4.5	14	35.5	31	79	48	122
2	50	5	15	38	32	81.5	49	124.5
2 1/2	65	6.5	16	40.5	33	84	50	127
3	75	7.5	17	43	34	86.5		
3 1/2	90	9	18	46	35	89		
4	100	10	19	48.5	36	91.5		
4 1/2	115	11.5	20	51	37	94		

KNITTING NEEDLES CONVERSION CHART

Canada/U.S.	0	1	2	3	4	5	6	7	8	9	10	10½	11	13	15
Metric (mm)	2	2¼	2¾	3¼	3½	3¾	4	4½	5	5½	6	6½	8	9	10

CROCHET HOOKS CONVERSION CHART

Canada/U.S.	1/B	2/C	3/D	4/E	5/F	6/G	8/H	9/I	10/J	10½/K	N
Metric (mm)	2.25	2.75	3.25	3.5	3.75	4.25	5	5.5	6	6.5	9.0

Exquisite Crochet Shawls is published by DRG, 306 East Parr Road, Berne, IN 46711. Printed in USA. Copyright © 2012 DRG.

RETAIL STORES: If you would like to carry this pattern book or any other DRG publications, visit DRGwholesale.com

Every effort has been made to ensure that the instructions in this publication are complete and accurate.
We cannot, however, take responsibility for human error, typographical mistakes or variations in individual work.
Please visit AnniesCustomerCare.com to check for pattern updates.

ISBN: 978-1-59635-424-1

1 2 3 4 5 6 7 8 9